Where Do Frogs Come From?

Where Do Frogs Come From?

Alex Vern

Green Light Readers
Harcourt, Inc.
San Diego   New York   London

www.harcourt.com

First Green Light Readers edition 2001
Green Light Readers is a trademark of Harcourt, Inc.,
registered in the United States of America and/or other jurisdictions.

Library of Congress Cataloging-in-Publication Data
Vern, Alex.
Where do frogs come from?/by Alex Vern.
p. cm.
"Green Light Readers."
1. Frogs—Development—Juvenile literature. [1. Tadpoles. 2. Frogs.]
I. Title. II. Series.
QL668.E2V47 2001
[E]—dc21   2001001481
ISBN 0-15-216304-2
ISBN 0-15-216296-8 (pb)

A C E G H F D B
A C E G H F D B (pb)

This big frog came from a small egg.

The black dots on this plant
are frog eggs.

Pop, pop, pop!

When a frog egg hatches,
a tadpole pops out.

At first, the tadpole has a long tail and a big body.

It looks for plants in the pond.
It eats the plants and grows very fast.

Soon the tadpole grows two strong back legs. They help it to kick and swim fast.

A tadpole has to swim
fast or a fish will eat it.

Small front legs form next.
The tadpole is almost a frog,
but it still has a tail.

At last the tail is gone.
The tadpole is now a
full-grown frog.

The frog is big and strong.
It can hop to find food or
run from danger.

Hop, hop!

The frog is also fast!
It eats lots of bugs.

Watch out fly!
Mmmm!

From Egg to Frog

1. Egg

2. Tadpole

3. Frog

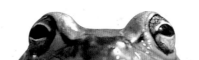